This journal belongs to

You are a beloved child of God,
precious to Him in every way. As you seek Him,
He will show you the mysteries of life and unfold
His unique plans for you—a life full of rich blessing.

God cares about you and knows all the desires of your heart.
He is as close as breathing. Let this journal inspire you
to express your thoughts, record your prayers,
embrace your dreams, and listen to what God is saying to you.

Be strong in the Lord, and may His peace
guide your heart always.

God made you so you could share in His creation,
could love and laugh and know Him.

TED GRIFFEN

This Is the Day

PROMISE JOURNAL

Ellie Claire
gift & paper expressions

...inspired by life

Live for Today

Live today! Live fully each moment of today. Trust God to let
you work through this moment and the next. He will give you
all you need. Don't skip over the painful or confusing moment—
even it has its important and rightful place in the day.

Today is unique! It has never occurred before, and it will
never be repeated. At midnight it will end, quietly, suddenly,
totally. Forever. But the hours between now and then
are opportunities with eternal possibilities.

CHARLES R. SWINDOLL

Let the whole earth sing to the LORD!
Each day proclaim the good news that he saves.

1 CHRONICLES 16:23 NLT

Thank You, Father, for the beautiful surprises you are planning
for me today. So often in my life an unexpected burst
of golden sunshine exploded through a black cloud, sending
inspiring shafts of warm, beautiful sunshine into my life.

ROBERT SCHULLER

We are weaving the future on the loom of today.

GRACE STRICKER DAWSON

Sunday 5-25-14

Went to Evangel Temple last
night and today and seen a
move of God. Nathan Morris
brought the word of God to
the church. He spoke on us
all having an upper room to
pray in. I really keep feeling
an acking in my heart for
the Yulee Church of God. I just
dont know what the Lord is
telling me. I'm just going to keep
praying for an answer. I do know
that God spoke to me last night
about me moving on in my
Ministrie and again today. I
just have to figure out if it's in
the Church of God or the
Assemblys of God. I know the
Lord will show me the way.
Praise God!

This is the day the LORD has made. We will rejoice and be glad in it.

PSALM 118:24 NLT

Blessings Await

Lift up your eyes. Your heavenly Father waits to bless you—
in inconceivable ways to make your life
what you never dreamed it could be.

ANNE ORTLUND

God can give you more blessings than you need.
Then you will always have plenty of everything—
enough to give to every good work.

2 CORINTHIANS 9:8 NCV

Blessed assurance, Jesus is mine!
Oh, what a foretaste of glory divine!
Heir of salvation, purchase of God,
Born of His Spirit, washed in His blood.

FANNY J. CROSBY

Jesus knows when a request comes to Him from the heart.
He has been waiting all along for us to bring our needy selves
to Him and receive from Him that eternal water.

DORIS GAILEY

Open your eyes
to the blessings around
See that beauty and
goodness surround you...
For you are God's pleasure
His flower of creation.

God's blessing makes life rich;
nothing we do can improve on God.

Through His Creation

In such a beautiful wilderness of wildflowers we are amused with
the very variety and novelty of the scene so much that we in our
pleasure lose all sense of weariness or fatigue in the length of our
wanderings and get to the end before we are aware of our journey.

JOHN CLARE

It is an extraordinary and beautiful thing that God, in creation...
works with the beauty of matter; the reality of things;
the discoveries of the senses, all five of them; so that we, in turn,
may hear the grass growing; see a face springing to life in love
and laughter.... The offerings of creation...our glimpses of truth.

MADELEINE L'ENGLE

I am convinced that God has built into all of us an appreciation
of beauty and has even allowed us to participate in the creation
of beautiful things and places. It may be one way God
brings healing to our brokenness, and a way that we can
contribute toward bringing wholeness to our fallen world.

MARY JANE WORDEN

Seeing how God works in nature can help us
understand how He works in our lives.

JANETTE OKE

*H*onor and majesty surround him;
strength and beauty fill his sanctuary.

PSALM 96:6 NLT

A Gift to Cherish

Everything in life is most fundamentally a gift.
And you receive it best, and you live it best,
by holding it with very open hands.

LEO O'DONOVAN

Stretch out your hand and take
the world's wide gift of Joy and Beauty.

CORINNE ROOSEVELT ROBINSON

Every day we live is a priceless gift of God, loaded with
possibilities to learn something new, to gain fresh insights.

DALE EVANS ROGERS

People should eat and drink and enjoy the fruits of their labor,
for these are gifts from God.

ECCLESIASTES 3:13 NLT

Your life is a gift from God,
And it is a privilege to share it.
Today and always,
Know that you have a
Very special place in others' hearts—
And in His.

God's free gift leads to our being made right with God.

ROMANS 5:16 NLT

Time is a very precious gift of God; so precious that
it's only given to us moment by moment.

AMELIA BARR

Fresh Faith

Lord...give me the gift of faith to be renewed and shared
with others each day. Teach me to live this moment only,
looking neither to the past with regret, nor the future
with apprehension. Let love be my aim and my life a prayer.

ROSEANN ALEXANDER-ISHAM

Know therefore that the LORD your God is God;
he is the faithful God, keeping his covenant of love to a thousand
generations of those who love him and keep his commands.

DEUTERONOMY 7:9 NIV

God will never, never, never let us down if we have faith...in Him.
He will always look after us. So we must cleave to Jesus.
Our whole life must simply be woven into Jesus.

MOTHER TERESA

The fruit of the Spirit is love, joy, peace, patience, kindness,
goodness, faithfulness, gentleness and self-control.

GALATIANS 5:22–23 NIV

Faith allows us to continually delight in life
since we have placed our needs in God's hands.

JANET L. WEAVER SMITH

Faith is not believing that God can—it's knowing that He will.

Faith is the confidence that what we hope for will actually happen; it gives us assurance about things we cannot see.

HEBREWS 11:1 NLT

Live a New Life

You have begun to live the new life, in which you
are being made new and are becoming like the One who made you.
This new life brings you the true knowledge of God.

COLOSSIANS 3:10 NCV

With God, life is eternal—both in quality and length.
There is no joy comparable to the joy of discovering
something new from God, about God. If the continuing life
is a life of joy, we will go on discovering, learning.

EUGENIA PRICE

Take on an entirely new way of life—a God-fashioned life,
a life renewed from the inside and working itself into your conduct
as God accurately reproduces his character in you.

EPHESIANS 4:23–24 MSG

Experience God in the breathless wonder and startling beauty
that is all around you. His sun shines warm upon your face.
His wind whispers in the treetops. Like the first rays
of morning light, celebrate the start of each day with God.

WENDY MOORE

Anyone who belongs to Christ has become a new person.
The old life is gone; a new life has begun!

2 CORINTHIANS 5:17 NLT

Enjoying His Presence

The Lord's chief desire is to reveal Himself to you and,
in order for Him to do that, He gives you abundant grace.
The Lord gives you the experience of enjoying His presence.
He touches you, and His touch is so delightful that,
more than ever, you are drawn inwardly to Him.

MADAME JEANNE GUYON

You're all I want in heaven! You're all I want on earth!...
I'm in the very presence of GOD—oh, how refreshing it is!
I've made Lord GOD my home.
GOD, I'm telling the world what you do!

PSALM 73:25 MSG

O the pure delight of a single hour
that before Thy throne I spend,
When I kneel in prayer, and with Thee, my God,
I commune as friend with friend!

FANNY J. CROSBY

Life need not be easy to be joyful.
Joy is not the absence of trouble,
but the presence of Christ.

WILLIAM VANDERHOVEN

*L*et the godly rejoice. Let them be glad in God's presence.
Let them be filled with joy.

PSALM 68:3 NLT

Our Gracious God

The LORD longs to be gracious to you;
he rises to show you compassion.
For the LORD is a God of justice.
Blessed are all who wait for him!

ISAIAH 30:18 NIV

His overflowing love delights to make us partakers
of the bounties He graciously imparts.

HANNAH MORE

O LORD, be gracious to us; we long for you. Be our strength
every morning, our salvation in time of distress.

ISAIAH 33:2 NIV

God makes everything come out right;
he puts victims back on their feet....
He doesn't endlessly nag and scold,
nor hold grudges forever.
He doesn't treat us as our sins deserve,
nor pay us back in full for our wrongs.
As high as heaven is over the earth,
so strong is his love to those who fear him.
And as far as sunrise is from sunset,
he has separated us from our sins.

PSALM 103:6, 9–12 MSG

*L*ord...give me only Your love and Your grace. With this I am
rich enough, and I have no more to ask.

IGNATIUS OF LOYOLA

A Sense of Wonder

Whether sixty or sixteen, there is in every human being's heart
the love of wonder, the sweet amazement at the stars
and starlike things, the undaunted challenge of events,
the unfailing childlike appetite for what-next,
and the joy of the game of living.

SAMUEL ULLMAN

Many, O LORD my God,
are the wonders which You have done,
And Your thoughts toward us;
There is none to compare with You
If I would declare and speak of them,
They would be too numerous to count.

PSALM 40:5 NASB

Dear Lord, grant me the grace of wonder. Surprise me,
amaze me, awe me in every crevice of Your universe.... Each day
enrapture me with Your marvelous things without number.
I do not ask to see the reason for it all; I ask only
to share the wonder of it all.

ABRAHAM JOSHUA HESCHEL

Loving Creator, help me reawaken my childlike sense of wonder
at the delights of Your world!

MARILYN MORGAN HELLEBERG

I will give thanks to the LORD with all my heart;
I will tell of all Your wonders.

PSALM 9:1 NASB

Good Gifts

Every good gift and every perfect gift is from above,
and comes down from the Father of lights, with whom
is no variation or shadow of turning.

JAMES 1:17 NKJV

God puts each fresh morning, each new chance of life,
into our hands as a gift.

Rejoice in the LORD your God! For the rain He sends
demonstrates His faithfulness. Once more the autumn rains
will come, as well as the rains of spring.

JOEL 2:23 NLT

I think miracles exist in part as gifts and in part as clues
that there is something beyond the flat world we see.

PEGGY NOONAN

He has not left Himself without testimony:
He has shown kindness by giving you rain from heaven
and crops in their seasons; he provides you with plenty of food
and fills your hearts with joy.

ACTS 14:17 NIV

Time, indeed, is a sacred gift, and each day is a little life.

SIR JOHN LUBBOCK

All perfect gifts are from above and all our blessings show
the amplitude of God's dear love which any heart may know.

Laura Lee Randall

A Heart Full of Praise

Let us give all that lies within us...to pure praise,
to pure loving adoration, and to worship from a grateful heart—
a heart that is trained to look up.

AMY CARMICHAEL

May you be filled with joy, always thanking the Father.
He has enabled you to share in the inheritance that belongs
to His people, who live in the light.

COLOSSIANS 1:11-12 NLT

Let's praise His name! He is holy, He is almighty. He is love.
He brings hope, forgiveness, heart cleansing, peace and power.
He is our deliverer and coming King. Praise His wonderful name!

LUCILLE M. LAW

The thought of You stirs us so deeply that we cannot be content
unless we praise You, because You have made us for Yourself
and our hearts find no peace until they rest in You.

AUGUSTINE

Let the message about Christ, in all its richness, fill your lives....
Sing psalms and hymns and spiritual songs to God
with thankful hearts.

COLOSSIANS 3:16 NLT

*A*ll who seek the LORD will praise Him.
Their hearts will rejoice with everlasting joy.

PSALM 22:26 NLT

Time to Enjoy

Slow down and enjoy life. It's not only the scenery
you miss by going too fast—you also miss the sense
of where you are going and why.

EDDIE CANTOR

Some days, it is enough encouragement just to watch the clouds
break up and disappear, leaving behind a blue patch of sky
and bright sunshine that is so warm upon my face.
It's a glimpse of divinity; a kiss from heaven.

Dear friend, I pray that you may enjoy good health and that all may
go well with you, even as your soul is getting along well.

3 JOHN 1:2 NIV

When we take time to notice the simple things in life, we never lack
for encouragement. We discover we are surrounded by a limitless
hope that's just wearing everyday clothes.

Find rest, O my soul, in God alone; my hope comes from him.

PSALM 62:5 NIV

Our hearts are not made happy by words alone.
We should seek a good and pure life, setting our minds
at rest and having confidence before God.

THOMAS À KEMPIS

*M*ost folks are about as happy as they make up their minds to be.

ABRAHAM LINCOLN

Glory in His Works

God is here! I hear His voice
While thrushes make the woods rejoice.
I touch His robe each time I place
My hand against a pansy's face.
I breathe His breath if I but pass
Verbenas trailing through the grass.
God is here! From every tree
His leafy fingers beckon me.

MADELEINE AARON

Wilderness and desert will sing joyously, the badlands
will celebrate and flower— Like the crocus in spring,
bursting into blossom, a symphony of song and color.
Mountain glories of Lebanon—a gift. Awesome Carmel,
stunning Sharon—gifts. God's resplendent glory, fully on display.
God awesome, God majestic.

ISAIAH 35:1–2 MSG

The tiniest dewdrop hanging from a grass blade in the morning
is big enough to reflect the sunshine and the blue of the sky.

GOD, brilliant Lord, yours is a household name.... I look up at your
macro-skies, dark and enormous, your handmade sky-jewelry,
moon and stars mounted in their settings.... GOD, brilliant Lord,
your name echoes around the world.

PSALM 8:1, 3, 9 MSG

*L*et the glory of the LORD endure forever;
let the LORD be glad in His works.

PSALM 104:31 NASB

The Best Times

When you open up the Bible and you pray the Scriptures
back to God, you're experiencing something really wonderful....
He's delighted. The silence confirms that we are His people.
We are talking and God is listening. But the best times are
when God starts talking, and we're quiet enough to hear Him.

CALVIN MILLER

God wants His children to establish such a close relationship
with Him that He becomes a natural partner in all
the experiences of life. That includes those precious, happy times.

GLORIA GAITHER

Come, let's worship him and bow down.
Let's kneel before the Lord who made us,
because he is our God
and we are the people he takes care of,
the sheep that he tends.
Today listen to what he says.

PSALM 95:6–7 NCV

The kiss of eternal life, and the warm embrace of God's Word,
are so sweet, and bring such pleasure, that you can never
become bored with them; you always want more.

HILDEGARD OF BINGEN

*I*t is God's love for us that He not only gives us His Word
but also lends us His ear.

DIETRICH BONHOEFFER

A Spirit of Joy

How necessary it is to cultivate a spirit of joy.... To act lovingly
is to begin to feel loving, and certainly to act joyfully
brings joy to others which in turn makes one feel joyful.
I believe we are called to the duty of delight.

DOROTHY DAY

Joy cannot be pursued. It comes from within.
It is a state of being. It does not depend on circumstances,
but triumphs over circumstances. It produces a gentleness
of spirit and a magnetic personality.

BILLY GRAHAM

God knows the rhythm of my spirit and knows my heart thoughts.
He is as close as breathing.

For the Kingdom of God is not a matter of what we eat or drink,
but of living a life of goodness and peace and joy in the Holy Spirit.

ROMANS 14:17 NLT

A joyful spirit is like a sunny day; it sheds a brightness
over everything; it sweetens our circumstances
and soothes our souls.

I know the LORD is always with me.
I will not be shaken, for he is right beside me.
No wonder my heart is glad, and I rejoice.

PSALM 16:8–9 NLT

Treasure Today

See each morning a world made anew, as if it were the morning
of the very first day;...treasure and use it,
as if it were the final hour of the very last day.

FAY HARTZELL ARNOLD

Celebrate God all day, every day. I mean, revel in him!
Make it as clear as you can to all you meet that you're on their side,
working with them and not against them. Help them see that the
Master is about to arrive.

PHILIPPIANS 4:4–5 MSG

Each day is a treasure box of gifts from God,
just waiting to be opened. Open your gifts with excitement.
You will find forgiveness attached to ribbons of joy.
You will find love wrapped in sparkling gems.

JOAN CLAYTON

Happy are those who hear the joyful call to worship,
for they will walk in the light of Your presence, LORD.

PSALM 89:15 NLT

In ordinary life we hardly realize that we receive a great deal more than we give, and that it is only with gratitude that life becomes rich.

DIETRICH BONHOEFFER

His Natural Wonders

It's simple things, like a glowing sunset, the sound
of a running stream, or the fresh smell in a meadow
that cause us to pause and marvel at the wonder of life,
to contemplate its meaning and significance. Who can hold
an autumn leaf in their hand, or sift the warm white sand
on the beach, and not wonder at the Creator of it all?

WENDY MOORE

What a wildly wonderful world, GOD!
You made it all, with Wisdom at your side,
made earth overflow with Your wonderful creations....
All the creatures look expectantly to you
to give them their meals on time.
You come, and they gather around;
You open your hand and they eat from it....
Take back your Spirit and they die....
Send out your Spirit and they spring to life.

PSALM 104:24, 27–30 MSG

Blue skies with white clouds on summer days. A myriad of stars
on clear moonlit nights. Tulips and roses and violets
and dandelions and daisies. Bluebirds and laughter
and sunshine and Easter. See how He loves us!

ALICE CHAPIN

*B*eauty puts a face on God. When we gaze at nature,
at a loved one, at a work of art, our soul immediately recognizes
and is drawn to the face of God.

MARGARET BROWNLEY

The Rhythms of Life

In waiting we begin to get in touch with the rhythms of life—
stillness and action, listening and decision. They are the rhythms
of God. It is in the everyday and the commonplace that we learn
patience, acceptance, and contentment.

RICHARD J. FOSTER

Love comes while we rest against our Father's chest.
Joy comes when we catch the rhythms of His heart.
Peace comes when we live in harmony with those rhythms.

KEN GIRE

In the process of creation and relationship, what seems mundane
and trivial may show itself to be holy, precious, part of a pattern.

LUCI SHAW

Nothing can give you quite the same thrill as the feeling
that you are in harmony with the great God of the universe
who created all things.

JAMES DOBSON

May God, who gives this patience and encouragement,
help you live in complete harmony with each other

ROMANS 15:5 NLT

*O*f all earthly music, that which reaches farthest into heaven
is the beating of a truly loving heart.

HENRY WARD BEECHER

Experience Christ

Once the seeking heart finds God in personal experience there will be no problem about loving Him. To know Him is to love Him and to know Him better is to love Him more.

A. W. TOZER

My beloved friends, let us continue to love each other since love comes from God. Everyone who loves is born of God and experiences a relationship with God.

1 JOHN 4:7 MSG

Peace is knowing you are right with God, you are right in your relationships, and you are living where God wants you to be—in His will.

JACK HAYFORD

Happiness is found in relationships. And life's greatest happiness is found in life's greatest relationship: a personal relationship with God through Jesus Christ.

KENNETH L. TANGEN

May you experience the love of Christ, though it is too great to understand fully. Then you will be made complete with all the fullness of life and power that comes from God.

EPHESIANS 3:19 NLT

*T*his is how we know what love is:
Jesus Christ laid down his life for us.

A Splendid Gift

This bright, new day, complete with twenty-four hours
of opportunities, choices, and attitudes comes with a perfectly
matched set of 1440 minutes. This unique gift, this one day,
cannot be exchanged, replaced or refunded. Handle with care.
Make the most of it. There is only one to a customer!

As each one has received a special gift, employ it in serving
one another as good stewards of the manifold grace of God.

1 PETER 4:10 NASB

You have a unique message to deliver, a unique song to sing,
a unique act of love to bestow. This message, this song, and this act
of love have been entrusted exclusively to the one and only you.

JOHN POWELL

May Jesus himself and God our Father, who reached out in love
and surprised you with gifts of unending help and confidence,
put a fresh heart in you, invigorate your work, enliven your speech.

2 THESSALONIANS 2:16–17 MSG

*L*ive your life while you have it.
Life is a splendid gift—there is nothing small about it.

FLORENCE NIGHTINGALE

Filled with God's Love

The heart is rich when it is content, and it is always content
when its desires are fixed on God. Nothing can bring
greater happiness than doing God's will for the love of God.

MIGUEL FEBRES CORDERO MUÑOZ

Bless the LORD, O my soul;
And all that is within me, bless His holy name!
Bless the LORD, O my soul,
And forget not all His benefits....
Who crowns you with lovingkindness and tender mercies,
Who satisfies your mouth with good things,
So that your youth is renewed like the eagle's.

PSALM 103:1–5 NKJV

When we trade with God we always come out a winner. Give Him
your heart of stone and He will give you in return, a heart of flesh—
one that is clean and filled with His love.

Let Jesus be in your heart,
Eternity in your spirit,
The world under your feet,
The will of God in your actions.
And let the love of God shine forth from you.

CATHERINE OF GENOA

$\mathcal{A}$ joyful heart is like a sunshine of God's love.... And if we pray,
we will become that sunshine of God's love—in our own home,
the place where we live, and in the world at large.

MOTHER TERESA

God Hears My Prayer

So wait before the Lord. Wait in the stillness. And in that stillness,
assurance will come to you. You will know that you are heard;
you will know that your Lord ponders the voice
of your humble desires; you will hear quiet words spoken to you
yourself, perhaps to your grateful surprise and refreshment.

AMY CARMICHAEL

I call on you, O God, for you will answer me;
give ear to me and hear my prayer.
Show the wonder of your great love.

PSALM 17:6–7 NIV

You can talk to God because God listens. Your voice matters
in heaven. He takes you very seriously. When you enter
His presence, the attendants turn to you to hear your voice.
No need to fear that you will be ignored. Even if you stammer
or stumble, even if what you have to say impresses no one,
it impresses God—and He listens.

MAX LUCADO

I prayed to the LORD, and He answered me.
He freed me from all my fears.
Those who look to Him for help will be radiant with joy.

PSALM 34:4–5 NLT

When we call on God, He bends down His ear to listen, as a father bends down to listen to his little child.

ELIZABETH CHARLES

Growing Joy

Joy is...deeper than an emotional expression of happiness.
Joy is a growing, evolving manifestation
of God in my life as I walk with Him.

BONNIE MONSON

Though you have not seen him, you love him.
Though you do not now see him, you believe in him and rejoice
with joy that is inexpressible and filled with glory.

1 PETER 1:8 ESV

It is pleasing to...God whenever you rejoice or laugh
from the bottom of your heart.

MARTIN LUTHER

Even when we cannot see the why and wherefore of God's dealings,
we know that there is love in and behind them,
and so we can rejoice always.

J. I. PACKER

The godly will rejoice in the LORD and find shelter in him.
And those who do what is right will praise him.

PSALM 64:10 NLT

Joy is really a road sign pointing us to God.
Once we have found God...we no longer need to trouble
ourselves so much about the quest for joy.

C. S. LEWIS

*L*et the heavens rejoice, let the earth be glad;
let them say among the nations, "The Lord reigns!"

1 CHRONICLES 16:31 NIV

Inspiration to Love

Look deep within yourself and recognize what brings life and grace
into your heart. It is this that can be shared with those around you.
You are loved by God. This is an inspiration to love.

CHRISTOPHER DE VINCK

To be grateful is to recognize the Love of God in everything He has
given us—and He has given us everything. Every breath we draw
is a gift of His love, every moment of existence is a gift of grace.

THOMAS MERTON

Thank you, Lord, for the grace of your love,
for the grace of friendship, and for the grace of beauty.

HENRI J. M. NOUWEN

Set your hope fully on the grace to be given you
when Jesus Christ is revealed.

1 PETER 1:13 NIV

The love of the Father is like a sudden rain shower
that will pour forth when you least expect it,
catching you up into wonder and praise.

RICHARD J. FOSTER

How ow great is the love the Father has lavished on us,
that we should be called children of God!

1 JOHN 3:1 NIV

A Life of Purpose

To be glad of life, because it gives you the chance to love and to
work and to play and to look up at the stars; to be satisfied with
your possessions, but not contented with yourself until you have
made the best of them;...to think seldom of your enemies,
often of your friends, and every day of Christ; and to spend
as much time as you can, with body and with spirit
in God's out-of-doors—these are little guideposts
on the footpath to peace.

HENRY VAN DYKE

The meaning of earthly existence lies, not as we have grown
used to thinking, in prospering, but in the development of the soul.

ALEKSANDR SOLZHENITSYN

"For I know the plans I have for you," declares the LORD,
"plans to prosper you and not to harm you,
plans to give you hope and a future."

JEREMIAH 29:11 NIV

Life begins each morning.... Each morning is the open door
to a new world—new vistas, new aims, new tryings.

LEIGH MITCHELL HODGES

*A*nd we know that all things work together for good to those
who love God, to those who are the called according to His purpose.

God with Us

God gets down on His knees among us; gets on our level
and shares Himself with us. He does not reside afar off
and send diplomatic messages, He kneels among us....
God shares Himself generously and graciously.

EUGENE PETERSON

We are of such value to God that He came to live among us...
and to guide us home. He will go to any length to seek us,
even to being lifted high upon the cross to draw us back to Himself.
We can only respond by loving God for His love.

CATHERINE OF SIENNA

God is our refuge and strength, an ever-present help in trouble.

PSALM 46:1 NIV

God loves to look at us, and loves it when we will
look back at Him. Even when we try to run away
from our troubles...God will find us, bless us, even when we
feel most alone, unsure.... God will find a way to let us know
that He is with us *in this place*, wherever we are.

KATHLEEN NORRIS

When all is said and done,
the last word is Immanuel—God-With-Us.

ISAIAH 8:10 MSG

*M*y Presence will go with you, and I will give you rest.

EXODUS 33:14 NIV

Abundant Life

To love by freely giving is its own reward. To be possessed by love
and to in turn give love away is to find the secret of abundant life.

GLORIA GAITHER

I have come that they may have life,
and that they may have it more abundantly.

JOHN 10:10 NKJV

Your deepest joy comes when you have nothing around you
to bring outward pleasure and Jesus becomes your total joy.

A. WETHERELL JOHNSON

There are only two ways to live your life.
One is as though nothing is a miracle.
The other is as though everything is a miracle.

RICHARD CRASHAW

The serene beauty of a holy life is the most powerful influence
in the world next to the power of God.

BLAISE PASCAL

May what our Master Jesus Christ gives freely
be deeply and personally yours, my friends.

GALATIANS 6:18 MSG

*N*ot what we have but what we enjoy constitutes our abundance.

JOHN PETIT-SENN

The Father's Delight

God is so big He can cover the whole world with His love,
and so small He can curl up inside your heart.

JUNE MASTERS BACHER

Isn't it a wonderful morning? The world looks like something God
had just imagined for His own pleasure.

LUCY MAUD MONTGOMERY

I praise you, Father, Lord of heaven and earth, because you have
hidden these things from the wise and learned, and revealed them
to little children. Yes, Father, for this was your good pleasure.

LUKE 10:21 NIV

Are you aware that the Father takes delight in you
and that He thinks about you all the time?

JACK FROST

I've loved you the way my Father has loved me.
Make yourselves at home in my love. If you keep my commands,
you'll remain intimately at home in my love. That's what I've done—
kept my Father's commands and made myself at home in his love.

JOHN 15:9 MSG

All the things in this world are gifts and signs of God's love to us.
The whole world is a love letter from God.

PETER KREEFT

Endless Wonders

A fiery sunset, tiny pansies by the wayside, the sound of raindrops
tapping on the roof—what extraordinary delight we find
in the simple wonders of life! With wide eyes and full hearts,
we may cherish what others often miss.

As we grow in our capacities to see and enjoy the joys
that God has placed in our lives, life becomes a glorious experience
of discovering His endless wonders.

WENDY MOORE

I will show wonders in the heavens and in the earth.

JOEL 2:30 NKJV

I still find each day too short for all the thoughts I want to think,
all the walks I want to take, all the books I want to read,
and all the friends I want to see. The longer I live, the more
my mind dwells upon the beauty and the wonder of the world.

JOHN BURROUGHS

The heavens proclaim the glory of God.
The skies display his craftsmanship.

PSALM 19:1 NLT

*G*od is the sunshine that warms us, the rain that melts the frost
and waters the young plants. The presence of God
is a climate of strong and bracing love, always there.

JOAN ARNOLD

Give Me Joy

God give me joy in the common things:
In the dawn that lures, the eve that sings...
In the springtime's spacious field of gold,
In the precious light by winter doled...
In the thought that life has love to spend,
In the faith that God's at journey's end.
God give me hope for each day that springs,
God give me joy in the common things!

THOMAS CURTIS CLARK

Half the joy of life is in little things taken on the run.
Let us run if we must—even the sands do that—but let us
keep our hearts young and our eyes open that nothing
worth our while shall escape us. And everything is worth its while
if we only grasp it and its significance.

VICTOR CHERBULIEZ

The joy that you give to others
is the joy that comes back to you.

JOHN GREENLEAF WHITTIER

The Lord is my strength and shield. I trust Him with all my heart.
He helps me, and my heart is filled with joy.

PSALM 28:7 NLT

Glorious Living

It's in Christ that we find out who we are and what
we are living for. Long before we first heard of Christ
and got our hopes up, he had his eye on us, had designs on us
for glorious living, part of the overall purpose he is working out
in everything and everyone.

EPHESIANS 1:11–12 MSG

All [God's] glory and beauty come from within,
and there He delights to dwell. His visits there are frequent,
His conversation sweet, His comforts refreshing,
His peace passing all understanding.

THOMAS À KEMPIS

Isn't everything you have and everything you are
sheer gifts from God?

1 CORINTHIANS 4:7 MSG

Each dawn holds a new hope for a new plan,
making the start of each day the start of a new life.

GINA BLAIR

To everything there is a season,
a time for every purpose under heaven.

ECCLESIASTES 3:1 NKJV

The patterns of our days are always rearranging...and each design
for living is unique, graced with its own special beauty.

His Beautiful World

The beauty of the earth, the beauty of the sky, the order
of the stars, the sun, the moon...their very loveliness
is their confession of God: for who made these lovely mutable things,
but He who is Himself unchangeable beauty?

AUGUSTINE

Creation and creatures applaud you, God;
your holy people bless you.
They talk about the glories of your rule,
they exclaim over your splendor....
Generous to a fault,
you lavish your favor on all creatures.
Everything God does is right—
the trademark on all his works is love.

PSALM 145:10–11, 16–17 MSG

The God who holds the whole world in His hands wraps Himself
in the splendor of the sun's light and walks among the clouds.

God's love is like a river springing up in the Divine Substance
and flowing endlessly through His creation, filling all things
with life and goodness and strength.

THOMAS MERTON

The best and most beautiful things in the world cannot be seen
or even touched. They must be felt with the heart.

HELEN KELLER

*S*omething deep in all of us yearns for God's beauty,
and we can find it no matter where we are.

SUE MONK KIDD

Time Well Spent

Mary...was sitting at Jesus' feet and listening to him teach.
But Martha was busy with all the work to be done.
She went in and said, "Lord, don't you care that my sister
has left me alone to do all the work? Tell her to help me."
But the Lord answered her, "Martha, Martha, you are worried
and upset about many things. Only one thing is important.
Mary has chosen the better thing, and it will never
be taken away from her."

LUKE 10:39–42 NCV

Being present with someone I love is never a waste of time,
especially if God is the one with whom I am present.
Martha complained about Mary wasting time at Jesus' feet
while work piled up.... Indeed, any time spent in prayer seems
wasted to someone who has priorities other than a relationship
with God. For one who loves God, however,
there is no more productive, or necessary, act.

PHILIP YANCEY

Life in the presence of God should be known to us
in conscious experience. It is a life to be enjoyed
every moment of every day.

A. W. TOZER

God is never in a hurry but spends years with those
He expects to greatly use.

L. B. COWMAN

Refreshed and Renewed

Your thoughts—how rare, how beautiful! God,
I'll never comprehend them! I couldn't even begin to count them—
any more than I could count the sand of the sea.
Oh, let me rise in the morning and live always with you!

PSALM 139:17 MSG

When we allow God the privilege of shaping our lives,
we discover new depths of purpose and meaning.
What a joyful thought to realize you are a chosen vessel for God—
perfectly suited for His use.

JONI EARECKSON TADA

But as for me, I shall sing of Your strength;
Yes, I shall joyfully sing of Your lovingkindness in the morning,
For You have been my stronghold.

PSALM 59:16 NASB

May our lives be illumined
by the steady radiance
renewed daily,
of a wonder,
the source of which
is beyond reason.

DAG HAMMARSKJÖLD

*S*ome blessings—like rainbows after rain
or a friend's listening ear—are extraordinary gifts
waiting to be discovered in an ordinary day.

The Ocean of God's Love

Your unfailing love, O Lord, is as vast as the heavens;
your faithfulness reaches beyond the clouds.
Your righteousness is like the mighty mountains,
your justice like the ocean depths....
How precious is your unfailing love, O God!

PSALM 36:5–7 NLT

Could we with ink the ocean fill
And were the skies of parchment made,
Were every stalk on earth a quill
And every man a scribe by trade
To write the love of God above
Would drain the ocean dry,
Nor could the scroll contain the whole
Tho' stretched from sky to sky.

FREDERICK M. LEHMAN

God loves you in the morning sun and the evening rain,
without caution or regret.

BRENNAN MANNING

You are in the Beloved...therefore infinitely dear to the Father,
unspeakably precious to Him.
You are never, not for one second, alone.

NORMAN DOWTY

The treasure our heart searches for
is found in the ocean of God's love.

JANET WEAVER SMITH

Praise Overflows

All enjoyment spontaneously overflows into praise....
The world rings with praise.... I think we delight to praise
what we enjoy because the praise not merely expresses
but completes the enjoyment; it is the appointed consummation.

C. S. LEWIS

Does not all nature around me praise God?
If I were silent, I should be an exception to the
universe. Does not the thunder praise Him as it rolls
like drums in the march of the God of armies?...
Does not the lightning write His name in letters of fire?
Has not the whole earth a voice?
And...can I silent be?

CHARLES H. SPURGEON

God's pursuit of praise from us and our pursuit of pleasure in Him
are one and the same pursuit. God's quest to be glorified
and our quest to be satisfied reach their goal in this one experience:
our delight in God which overflows in praise.

JOHN PIPER

Sing praises to God, sing praises; sing praises to our King, sing praises.
For God is the King of all the earth; sing to him a psalm of praise.

PSALM 47:6–7 NIV

Truly Blessed

Blessed are those you choose and bring near to live in your courts!
We are filled with the good things of your house,
of your holy temple.

PSALM 65:4 NIV

Have you ever thought that in every action of grace in your heart
you have the whole omnipotence of God engaged to bless you?

ANDREW MURRAY

You can be sure that God will take care of everything you need,
his generosity exceeding even yours in the glory that pours
from Jesus. Our God and Father abounds in glory
that just pours out into eternity.

PHILIPPIANS 4:18 MSG

In difficulties, I can drink freely of God's power
and experience His touch of refreshment and blessing—
much like an invigorating early spring rain.

ANABEL GILLHAM

From his abundance we have all received
one gracious blessing after another.

JOHN 1:16 NLT

Our God is so wonderfully good, and lovely, and blessed
in every way that the mere fact of belonging to Him is enough
for an untellable fullness of joy!

HANNAH WHITALL SMITH

Delight in the Lord

Take delight in the LORD,
and He will give you your heart's desires.
Commit everything you do to the LORD.
Trust Him, and He will help you.
He will make your innocence radiate like the dawn,
and the justice of your cause will shine like the noonday sun.

PSALM 37:4–6 NLT

Love is the response of the heart to the overwhelming
goodness of God.... You may be so awestruck and full of love
at His presence that words do not come.

RICHARD J. FOSTER

Send forth your light and your truth,
let them guide me;
let them bring me to your holy mountain,
to the place where you dwell.
Then will I go to the altar of God,
to God, my joy and my delight.

PSALM 43:3–4 NIV

Joy is perfect acquiesce in God's will because
the soul delights itself in God Himself.

H. W. WEBB-PEPLOE

Few delights can equal the mere presence
of one whom we trust utterly.

GEORGE MACDONALD

Footpath to Peace

God came to us because God wanted to join us on the road,
to listen to our story, and to help us realize that we are not
walking in circles but moving toward the house of peace and joy.

HENRI J. M. NOUWEN

Peace I leave with you, My peace I give to you;
not as the world gives do I give to you. Let not your heart
be troubled, neither let it be afraid.

JOHN 14:27 NKJV

Only God gives true peace—a quiet gift He sets within us
just when we think we've exhausted our search for it.

You will keep in perfect peace all who trust in you,
all whose thoughts are fixed on you!

ISAIAH 26:3 NLT

Peace *with* God brings the peace *of* God.
It is a peace that settles our nerves, fills our mind,
floods our spirit, and in the midst of the uproar around us,
gives us the assurance that everything is all right.

BOB MUMFORD

God's peace is joy resting. His joy is peace dancing.

F. F. BRUCE

Joy Comes from Within

Joy cannot be pursued. It comes from within.
It is a state of being. It does not depend on circumstances,
but triumphs over circumstances. It produces a gentleness
of spirit and a magnetic personality.

BILLY GRAHAM

Joyful is the person who finds wisdom,
the one who gains understanding.

PROVERBS 3:13 NLT

The God of the universe—the One who created everything
and holds it all in His hands—created each of us in His image,
to bear His likeness, His imprint. It is only when Christ dwells
within our hearts, radiating the pure light of His love
through our humanity that we discover who we are and what we
were intended to be. There is no other joy that reaches as deep
or as wide or as high—there is no other joy that is more complete.

WENDY MOORE

The miracle of joy is this: It happens when there is no apparent
reason for it. Circumstances may call for despair. Yet something
different rouses itself inside us.... We remember God.
We remember He is love. We remember He is near.

RUTH SENTER

The Lord has filled my heart with joy.

1 SAMUEL 2:1 NCV

God Loves You

Just as there comes a warm sunbeam into every cottage window,
so comes a love-beam of God's care for every separate need.

NATHANIEL HAWTHORNE

It is clear to us, friends, that God not only loves you very much
but also has put His hand on you for something special.

1 THESSALONIANS 1:4 MSG

Listening to God is a firsthand experience.... God invites *you* to
vacation in His splendor. He invites *you* to feel the touch
of His hand. He invited *you* to feast at His table.
He wants to spend time with *you*.

MAX LUCADO

I've called your name. You're mine.
When you're in over your head, I'll be there with you....
When you're between a rock and a hard place,
it won't be a dead end—
Because I am God, your personal God,
The Holy of Israel, your Savior.
I paid a huge price for you....
That's how much you mean to me!
That's how much I love you!

ISAIAH 43:1–3 MSG

Open your hearts to the love God instills....
God loves you tenderly. What He gives you is not to be kept
under lock and key, but to be shared.

MOTHER TERESA

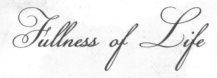

Fullness of Life

Gratitude unlocks the fullness of life. It turns what we have
into enough, and more.... It can turn a meal into a feast, a house
into a home, a stranger into a friend. It turns problems into gifts,
failures into successes, the unexpected into perfect timing,
and mistakes into important events.

MELODY BEATTIE

You've always given me breathing room, a place to
get away from it all, a lifetime pass to your safe-house,
an open invitation as your guest.

PSALM 61:3 MSG

I think what we're longing for is not "the good life" as it's been
advertised to us...but life in its fullness, its richness, its abundance.
Living more reflectively helps us enter into that fullness.

KEN GIRE

I pray that from his glorious, unlimited resources he will empower
you with inner strength through his Spirit. Then Christ will make
his home in your hearts as you trust in him. Your roots will grow
down into God's love and keep you strong.

EPHESIANS 3:16–17 NLT

*L*ove wholeheartedly, be surprised, give thanks and praise—
then you will discover the fullness of your life.

DAVID STEINDL-RAST

Thirst for More

O God, you are my God;
I earnestly search for you.
My soul thirsts for you;
my whole body longs for you
in this parched and weary land
where there is no water.
I have seen you in your sanctuary
and gazed upon your power and glory.
Your unfailing love is better than life itself.

PSALM 63:1–3 NLT

Whatever it is,
However impossible it seems,
Whatever the obstacles that stand between you and it,
If it is noble, if it is consistent with God's kingdom,
You must hunger after it
And stretch yourself to reach it.

CHARLES COHN

All things are created by God and therefore good. All that is
desirable in things is an image of the supremely desirable God....
There is simply nothing else to desire except God or God's
images and reflections.... All the different things we desire
are really one; for they are reflections of aspects of God.

PETER KREEFT

Genuine heart-hunger, accompanied by sincere seeking
after eternal values, does not go unrewarded.

JUSTINE KNIGHT

*B*lessed are those who hunger and thirst
for righteousness, for they will be filled.

The Wonder of Living

When I need a dose of wonder I wait for a clear night and go look
for the stars.... In the country the great river of the Milky Way
streams across the sky, and I know that our planet is a small part
of that river of stars.... Often the wonder of the stars is enough to
return me to God's loving grace.

MADELEINE L'ENGLE

Normal day, let me be aware of the treasure you are. Let me learn
from you, love you, bless you before you depart. Let me not pass you
by in quest of some rare and perfect tomorrow.

We need to recapture the power of imagination; we shall find that
life can be full of wonder, mystery, beauty, and joy.

SIR HAROLD SPENCER JONES

The wonder of living is held within the beauty of silence,
the glory of sunlight...the sweetness of fresh spring air,
the quiet strength of earth, and the love that lies
at the very root of all things.

The heavens praise your wonders, O LORD,
your faithfulness too, in the assembly of the holy ones.

PSALM 89:5 NIV

Significant to Him

The God who created, names, and numbers the stars in the heavens
also numbers the hairs of my head.... He pays attention to
very big things and to very small ones. What matters to me
matters to Him, and that changes my life.

ELISABETH ELLIOT

The LORD will guide you always; He will satisfy your needs in a
sun-scorched land and will strengthen your frame. You will be like a
well-watered garden, like a spring whose waters never fail.

ISAIAH 58:11 NIV

What matters supremely is not the fact that I know God,
but the larger fact which underlies it—the fact that He knows me....
I am never out of His mind.... I know Him because
He first knew me, and continues to know me.

J. I. PACKER

I'm not saying that I have this all together, that I have it made.
But I am well on my way, reaching out for Christ,
who has so wondrously reached out for me.

PHILIPPIANS 3:12 MSG

*T*uck [this] thought into your heart today. Treasure it. Your Father
God cares about your daily everythings that concern you.

KAY ARTHUR

Paths of Life

The path of the righteous is like the light of dawn, that shines
brighter and brighter until the full day.

PROVERBS 4:18 NASB

A new path lies before us;
We're not sure where it leads;
But God goes on before us,
Providing all our needs.
This path, so new, so different
Exciting as we climb,
Will guide us in His perfect will
Until the end of time.

LINDA MAURICE

The best things are nearest...light in your eyes, flowers at your feet,
duties at your hand, the path of God just before you.

ROBERT LOUIS STEVENSON

God's bright sunshine overhead,
God's flowers beside your feet...
And by such pleasant pathways led,
May all your life be sweet.

HELEN WAITHMAN

Come, let us go up to the mountain of the LORD.... There he will
teach us his ways, and we will walk in his paths.

MICAH 4:2 NLT

*Y*our word is a lamp to my feet and a light to my path.

PSALM 119:105 NKJV

Full of Laughter

Wholehearted, ready laughter heals, encourages, relaxes anyone
within hearing distance. The laughter that springs from love makes
wide the space around it—gives room for the loved one to enter in.
Real laughter welcomes, and never shuts out.

EUGENIA PRICE

When the righteous see God in action they'll laugh,
they'll sing, they'll laugh and sing for joy.
Sing hymns to God; all heaven, sing out.

PSALM 68:3–4 MSG

Sense of humor; God's great gift
causes spirits to uplift,
Helps to make our bodies mend;
lightens burdens; cheers a friend;
Tickles children; elders grin
at this warmth that glows within;
Surely in the great hereafter
heaven must be full of laughter!

Humor is one of God's most marvelous gifts. Humor gives us
smiles, laughter, and gaiety. Humor reveals the roses and hides
the thorns. Humor makes our heavy burdens light
and smooths the rough spots in our pathways.

SAM ERVIN

*H*e will yet fill your mouth with laughter
and your lips with shouts of joy.

Made for Joy

Our hearts were made for joy. Our hearts were made to enjoy
the One who created them. Too deeply planted to be much affected
by the ups and downs of life, this joy is a knowing and a being
known by our Creator. He sets our hearts alight with radiant joy.

For You, O LORD, have made me glad by what You have done,
I will sing for joy at the works of Your hands.

PSALM 92:4 NASB

O God, I have tasted Thy goodness,
and it has both satisfied me and made me thirsty for more.

A.W. TOZER

You have made known to me the path of life; you will fill me with joy
in your presence, with eternal pleasures at your right hand.

PSALM 16:11 NIV

Live for today but hold your hands open to tomorrow.
Anticipate the future and its changes with joy. There is a seed
of God's love in every event, every circumstance,
every unpleasant situation in which you may find yourself.

BARBARA JOHNSON

The joy of the Lord is your strength.

NEHEMIAH 8:10 NKJV

New Every Morning

Always new. Always exciting. Always full of promise.
The mornings of our lives, each a personal daily miracle!

GLORIA GAITHER

A quiet morning with a loving God puts the events
of the upcoming day into proper perspective.

JANETTE OKE

The faithful love of the LORD never ends! His mercies never cease.
Great is his faithfulness; his mercies begin afresh each morning.

LAMENTATIONS 3:22–23 NLT

In the morning let our hearts gaze upon God's love
and the love He has allowed us to share, and in the beauty
of that vision, let us go forth to meet the day.

ROY LESSIN

It is good to give thanks to the LORD and to sing praises
to Your name, O Most High; to declare Your lovingkindness
in the morning and Your faithfulness by night.

PSALM 92:1–2 NASB

That is God's call to us—simply to be people who are content
to live close to Him and to renew the kind of life
in which the closeness is felt and experienced.

THOMAS MERTON

*Satisfy us in the morning with your unfailing love,
that we may sing for joy and be glad all our days.*

PSALM 90:14 NIV

Boundless Strength

Think excitement, talk excitement, act out excitement,
and you are bound to become an excited person.
Life will take on a new zest, deeper interest and greater meaning.
You can think, talk and act yourself into dullness or into monotony
or into unhappiness. By the same process you can build up
inspiration, excitement and a surging depth of joy.

NORMAN VINCENT PEALE

Hope floods my heart with delight!
Running on air, mad with life, dizzy, reeling,
Upward I mount—faith is sight, life is feeling,
Hope is the day-star of might!

MARGARET WITTER FULLER

From the fullness of his grace
we have all received
one blessing after another.

JOHN 1:16 NIV

God's holy beauty comes near you, like a spiritual scent, and it
stirs your drowsing soul.... He creates in you the desire to find Him
and run after Him—to follow wherever He leads you, and to press
peacefully against His heart wherever He is.

JOHN OF THE CROSS

$\mathcal{O}$h, the utter extravagance of his work in us who trust him—
endless energy, boundless strength!

EPHESIANS 1:19 MSG

Our Provider

The Lord is the everlasting God, the Creator of all the earth.
He never grows weak or weary. No one can measure the depths
of his understanding.... Even youths will become weak and tired,
and young men will fall in exhaustion. But those who trust
in the LORD will find new strength. They will soar high
on wings like eagles. They will run and not grow weary.
They will walk and not faint.

ISAIAH 40:28, 30–31 NLT

Just when we least expect it, [God] intrudes into our neat
and tidy notions about who He is and how He works.

JONI EARECKSON TADA

God takes care of His own. He knows our needs.... He stands ready
to come to our rescue. And at just the right moment He steps in and
proves Himself as our faithful heavenly Father.

CHARLES R. SWINDOLL

Joy comes from knowing God loves me and knows who I am and
where I'm going...that my future is secure as I rest in Him.

JAMES DOBSON

*H*ow great are your works, O Lord,
how profound your thoughts!

PSALM 92:5 NIV

Grace For Each Day

When we focus on God, the scene changes. He's in control
of our lives; nothing lies outside the realm of His redemptive grace.
Even when we make mistakes, fail in relationships, or deliberately
make bad choices, God can redeem us.

PENELOPE J. STOKES

God has not promised skies always blue,
flower-strewn pathways all our lives through;
God has not promised sun without rain,
joy without sorrow, peace without pain.
But God has promised strength for the day,
rest for the labor, light for the way,
grace for the trials, help from above,
unfailing sympathy, undying love.

ANNIE JOHNSON FLINT

He is the Source. Of everything. Strength for your day.
Wisdom for your task. Comfort for your soul. Grace for your battle.
Provision for each need. Understanding for each failure.
Assistance for every encounter.

JACK HAYFORD

God is sheer mercy and grace; not easily angered, He's rich in love.

PSALM 103:8 MSG

*T*oday I'll remember that, by God's grace,
I am all I need to be.

Attitude Is Everything

The wonder of our Lord is that He is so accessible to us
in the common things of our lives: the cup of water...
breaking of the bread...welcoming children into our arms...
fellowship over a meal...giving thanks. A simple attitude of caring,
listening, and lovingly telling the truth.

NANCIE CARMICHAEL

A positive attitude may not solve all your problems,
but it will annoy enough people to make it worth the effort.

HERM ALBRIGHT

If you have any encouragement from being united with Christ,
if any comfort from his love, if any fellowship with the Spirit,
if any tenderness and compassion, then make my joy complete
by being like-minded, having the same love, being one in spirit
and purpose. Do nothing out of selfish ambition or vain conceit,
but in humility consider others better than yourselves.

PHILIPPIANS 2:1–3 NIV

I have learned from experience that the greater part
of our happiness or misery depends on our dispositions
and not on our circumstances.

MARTHA WASHINGTON

A strong positive mental attitude will create
more miracles than any wonder drug.

PATRICIA NEAL

New Possibilities

What we feel, think, and do this moment influences
both our present and the future in ways we may never know.
Begin. Start right where you are. Consider your possibilities
and find inspiration...to add more meaning and zest to your life.

ALEXANDRA STODDARD

You see things as they are and ask, "Why?"
I dream things as they never were and ask, "Why not?"

GEORGE BERNARD SHAW

With man this is impossible, but with God all things are possible.

MATTHEW 19:26 NIV

Every time Jesus sees that there is a possibility of giving us
more than we know how to ask, He does so.

OLE HALLESBY

GOD made my life complete when I placed all the pieces
before him.... He gave me a fresh start.

2 SAMUEL 22:21 MSG

Start by doing what's necessary, then what's possible
and suddenly you are doing the impossible.

FRANCIS OF ASSISI

*The uncertainties of the present always give way
to the enchanted possibilities of the future.*

GELSEY KIRKLAND

I Found Loveliness

I found loveliness today
Down along life's broad highway—
Saw its beauty in the trees,
Heard it whisper in the breeze,
Felt its warmth in glad sunshine,
Rhythm caught in swaying pine—
All along life's broad highway
I found loveliness today.

I found loveliness today
Down along life's broad highway—
Beauty within pastures green,
Next in clouds of silvery sheen,
Golden glow at break of day,
Joy in children at their play,
Scented odor of wild rose;
Peace I found where violet grows—
All along life's broad highway
I found loveliness today.

CARLETON EVERETT KNOX

How lovely on the mountains are the feet of him
who brings good news, who announces peace and brings
good news of happiness.

ISAIAH 52:7 NASB

The innocent brightness of a new born day is lovely yet.

WILLIAM WORDSWORTH

How ow lovely are Your dwelling places, O LORD of hosts!
My soul longed and even yearned for the courts of the LORD.

PSALM 84:1–2 NASB

Living Water

Kindness has been described in many ways.
It is the poetry of the heart, the music of the world.
It is the golden chain which binds society together.
It is a fountain of gladness.

From God, great and small, rich and poor, draw living water
from a living spring, and those who serve Him freely and gladly
will receive grace answering to grace.

THOMAS À KEMPIS

We must drink deeply from the very Source the deep calm
and peace of interior quietude and refreshment of God,
allowing the pure water of divine grace to flow plentifully
and unceasingly from the Source itself.

MOTHER TERESA

Whoever believes in me, as the Scripture has said,
streams of living water will flow from within him.

JOHN 7:38 NIV

You never can measure what God will do through you if you
are rightly related to Jesus Christ. Keep your relationship right
with Him, then whatever circumstances you are in,
and whoever you meet day by day, He is pouring rivers
of living water through you.

OSWALD CHAMBERS

A kind heart is a fountain of gladness,
making everything in its vicinity freshen into smiles.

WASHINGTON IRVING

New Life of Love

So, chosen by God for this new life of love, dress in the wardrobe
God picked out for you: compassion, kindness, humility,
quiet strength, discipline. Be even-tempered,
content with second place, quick to forgive an offense.
Forgive as quickly and completely as the Master forgave you.
And regardless of what else you put on, wear love. It's your basic,
all-purpose garment. Never be without it.

COLOSSIANS 3:12–14 MSG

The light of God surrounds me;
The love of God enfolds me;
The power of God protects me;
The presence of God watches over me.
Wherever I am, God is.

At the very heart and foundation of all God's dealings with us...we
must dare to believe in and assert the infinite, unmerited,
and unchanging love of God.

L. B. COWMAN

Faith in God gives your life a center from which you can
reach out and dare to love the world.

BARBARA FARMER

You will find as you look back upon your life, that the moments
when you have really lived are the moments when you
have done things in the spirit of love.

HENRY DRUMMOND

*L*ove others for the sake of God.
Love God for His own sake.

AUGUSTINE

Really Alive

How beautiful it is to be alive!
To wake each morn as if the Maker's grace
Did us afresh from nothingness derive,
That we might sing "How happy is our case!
How beautiful it is to be alive."

HENRY SEPTIMUS SUTTON

Surely your goodness and unfailing love will pursue me all the days
of my life, and I will live in the house of the LORD forever.

PSALM 23:6 NLT

Isn't it splendid to think of all the things there are to find out about?
It just makes me feel glad to be alive—it's such an interesting world.
It wouldn't be half so interesting if we knew all about everything.

LUCY MAUD MONTGOMERY

The person in right standing before God through loyal
and steady believing is fully alive, really alive.

HABAKKUK 2:4 MSG

The LORD will command His lovingkindness in the daytime;
and His song will be with me in the night, a prayer to the God of my life.

PSALM 42:8 NASB

The Music of God

From the heart of God comes the strongest rhythm—the rhythm
of love. Without His love reverberating in us, whatever we do will
come across like a noisy gong or a clanging symbol. And so the
work of the human heart, it seems to me, is to listen for that music
and pick up on its rhythms.

KEN GIRE

He speaks, and the sound of his voice
is so sweet the birds hush their singing.
And the melody that he gave to me
within my heart is ringing.
And he walks with me, and he talks with me,
and he tells me I am his own.
And the joy we share as we tarry there
none other has ever known.

C. AUSTIN MILES

Life is what we are alive to. It is not length but breadth....
Be alive to...goodness, kindness, purity, love, history, poetry,
music, flowers, stars, God, and eternal hope.

MALTBIE D. BABCOCK

Let God have you, and let God love you—and don't be surprised if
your heart begins to hear music you've never heard and your feet
learn to dance as never before.

MAX LUCADO

Sing songs to the tune of his glory,
set glory to the rhythms of his praise.

PSALM 66:2 MSG

Blessed Assurance

Regardless of whether we feel strong or weak in our faith,
we remember that our assurance is not based upon our ability
to conjure up some special feeling. Rather, it is built upon
a confident assurance in the faithfulness of God. We focus on
His trustworthiness and especially on His steadfast love.

RICHARD J. FOSTER

In those times I can't seem to find God,
I rest in the assurance He knows how to find me.

NEVA COYLE

Do not be anxious about anything, but in everything, by prayer
and petition, with thanksgiving, present your requests to God.
And the peace of God, which transcends all understanding,
will guard your hearts and your minds in Christ Jesus.

PHILIPPIANS 4:6–7 NIV

To believe in God starts with a conclusion about Him,
develops into confidence in Him, and then matures
into a conversation with Him.

STUART BRISCOE

Faith is a living, daring confidence in God's grace, so sure and
certain that a man could stake his life on it a thousand times.

MARTIN LUTHER

*B*e assured, if you walk with Him and look to Him
and expect help from Him, He will never fail you.

GEORGE MUELLER

Joys of Living

God created us with an overwhelming desire to soar.
Our desire to develop and use every ounce of potential
He's placed in us is not egotistical. He designed us to be
tremendously productive and "to mount up with wings like eagles,"
realistically dreaming of what He can do with our potential.

CAROL KENT

Shout joyfully to the LORD, all the earth;
Break forth and sing for joy and sing praises.

PSALM 98:4 NASB

Oh, the wild joys of living!
The leaping from rock up to rock...
How good is man's life, the mere living!
How fit to employ
All the heart and the soul
And the senses forever in joy!

ROBERT BROWNING

If one is joyful, it means that one is faithfully living for God,
and that nothing else counts; and if one gives joy to others one is
doing God's work. With joy without and joy within, all is well.

JANET ERSKINE STUART

*C*hrist's love has moved me to such extremes. His love has
the first and last word in everything we do.

2 CORINTHIANS 5:13 MSG

Wonderfully Made

Each one of us is God's special work of art. Through us,
He teaches and inspires, delights and encourages, informs
and uplifts all those who view our lives. God, the master artist,
is most concerned about expressing Himself—His thoughts
and His intentions—through what He paints in our character....
[He] wants to paint a beautiful portrait of His Son
in and through your life. A painting like no other in all of time.

JONI EARECKSON TADA

I will give thanks to You, for I am fearfully and wonderfully made;
Wonderful are Your works,
And my soul knows it very well....
How precious also are Your thoughts to me, O God!
How vast is the sum of them!

PSALM 139:14, 17 NASB

We have been in God's thought from all eternity,
and in His creative love, His attention never leaves us.

MICHAEL QUOIST

Know that the LORD is God. It is he who made us,
and we are his; we are his people, the sheep of his pasture.

PSALM 100:3 NIV

The Attention of God

God is every moment totally aware of each one of us.
Totally aware in intense concentration and love.... No one passes
through any area of life, happy or tragic,
without the attention of God.

EUGENIA PRICE

If you are seeking after God, you may be sure of this:
God is seeking you much more. He is the Lover, and you
are His beloved. He has promised Himself to you.

JOHN OF THE CROSS

God possesses infinite knowledge and an awareness
which is uniquely His. At all times...I can realize that He knows,
loves, watches, understands, and more than that, He has a purpose.

BILLY GRAHAM

It is God's knowledge of me, His careful husbanding of the
ground of my being, His constant presence in the garden
of my little life that guarantees my joy.

W. PHILLIP KELLER

There is no peace like the peace of those whose minds
are possessed with full assurance that they have known God,
and God has known them.

J. I. PACKER

*M*ay you have the power to understand, as all God's people
should, how wide, how long, how high, and how deep his love is.

EPHESIANS 3:18 NLT

Real Joy

There is no greater joy nor greater reward
than to make a fundamental difference in someone's life.

MARY ROSE MCGEADY

I delight greatly in the LORD; my soul rejoices in my God.
For he has clothed me with garments of salvation
and arrayed me in a robe of righteousness.

ISAIAH 61:10 NIV

Joy is not happiness so much as gladness; it is the ecstasy
of eternity in a soul that has made peace with God
and is ready to do His will.

Real joy comes not from ease or riches or from the praise of men,
but from doing something worthwhile.

SIR WILFRED GRENFELL

I've grown to realize the joy
that comes from little victories is preferable to the fun
that comes from ease and the pursuit of pleasure.

LAWANA BLACKWELL

Joyful are people of integrity,
who follow the instructions of the LORD.
Joyful are those who obey his laws
and search for him with all their hearts.

PSALM 119:1–2 NLT

$\mathcal{G}$od's friendship is the unexpected joy we find
when we reach for His outstretched hand.

JANET L. WEAVER SMITH

The Presence of God

The simple fact of being...in the presence of the Lord
and of showing Him all that I think, feel, sense, and experience,
without trying to hide anything, must please Him.
Somehow, somewhere, I know that He loves me, even though I do
not feel that love as I can feel a human embrace, even though I do
not hear a voice as I hear human words of consolation....
God is greater than my senses, greater than my thoughts,
greater than my heart. I do believe that He touches me in places
that are unknown even to myself.

HENRI J. M. NOUWEN

I look behind me and you're there,
then up ahead and you're there, too—
your reassuring presence, coming and going.
This is too much, too wonderful—
I can't take it all in!

PSALM 139:5–6 MSG

A living, loving God can and does make His presence felt,
can and does speak to us in the silence of our hearts,
can and does warm and caress us till we no longer doubt
that He is near, that He is here.

BRENNAN MANNING

Know by the light of faith that God is present, and be content with directing all your actions toward Him.

BROTHER LAWRENCE

Infinite Goodness

All we are and all we have is by the...love of God!
The goodness of God is infinitely more wonderful
than we will ever be able to comprehend.

A. W. TOZER

Open your mouth and taste, open your eyes and see—
how good GOD is. Blessed are you who run to him.
Worship GOD if you want the best;
worship opens doors to all his goodness.

PSALM 34:8–9 MSG

All that is good, all that is true, all that is beautiful,
all that is beneficent, be it great or small,
be it perfect or fragmentary, natural as well as supernatural,
moral as well as material, comes from God.

JOHN HENRY NEWMAN

We walk without fear, full of hope and courage and strength
to do His will, waiting for the endless good which He is always
giving as fast as He can get us able to take it in.

GEORGE MACDONALD

The LORD is merciful and compassionate...
and filled with unfailing love.... The LORD always keeps his promises;
he is gracious in all he does.

PSALM 145:8–9, 13 NLT

God's Eternal Love

God, who is love—who is, if I may say it this way,
made out of love—simply cannot help but shed
blessing on blessing upon us.
We do not need to beg, for He simply cannot help it!

HANNAH WHITALL SMITH

The LORD is like a father to his children,
tender and compassionate to those who fear him....
The love of the LORD remains forever.

PSALM 103:13, 17 NLT

The reason we can dare to risk loving others is that "God has for
Christ's sake loved us." Think of it! We are loved eternally, totally,
individually, unreservedly! Nothing can take God's love away.

GLORIA GAITHER

Great is his love toward us,
and the faithfulness of the LORD endures forever.

PSALM 117:2 NIV

The impetus of God's love comes from within Himself, to share with
us His life and love. It is a beautiful, eternal gift, held out to us in
the hands of love. All we have to do is say "Yes!"

JOHN POWELL

*L*ove has its source in God, for love
is the very essence of His being.

KAY ARTHUR

A Spirit of Hope

I pray that God, the source of hope, will fill you completely with joy
and peace because you trust in Him. Then you will overflow with
confident hope through the power of the Holy Spirit.

ROMANS 15:13 NLT

Because You live, O Christ,
the spirit bird of hope is freed for flying,
our cages of despair no longer keep us
closed and life-denying.

SHIRLEY ERENA MURRAY

Show me your ways, O LORD...guide me in your truth
and teach me, for you are God my Savior, and my hope
is in you all day long. Remember, O LORD, your great mercy
and love.... According to your love remember me,
for you are good, O LORD.

PSALM 25:4–7 NIV

For I am bound with fleshly bands,
Joy, beauty, lie beyond my scope;
I strain my heart, I stretch my hands,
And catch at hope.

CHRISTINA ROSSETTI

In the presence of hope—faith is born. In the presence of faith, love becomes a possibility! In the presence of love—miracles happen!

ROBERT SCHULLER

A Centered Life

Life from the Center is a life of unhurried peace and power.
It is simple. It is serene.... We need not get frantic.
He is at the helm. And when our little day is done,
we lie down quietly in peace, for all is well.

THOMAS R. KELLY

Drop thy still dews of quietness
till all our strivings cease;
take from our souls the strain and stress,
and let our ordered lives confess
the beauty of Thy peace.

JOHN GREENLEAF WHITTIER

Because we are spiritual beings...it is for our good,
individually and collectively, to live our lives
in interactive dependence upon God.

DALLAS WILLARD

For of Him and through Him and to Him are all things,
to whom be glory forever. Amen.

ROMANS 11:36 NKJV

There is nothing but God's grace. We walk upon it;
we breathe it; we live and die by it;
it makes the nails and axles of the universe.

ROBERT LOUIS STEVENSON

For in him we live and move and have our being.

ACTS 17:28 NIV

Go Out with Joy

Into all our lives, in many simple, familiar, homely ways,
God infuses this element of joy from the surprises of life,
which unexpectedly brighten our days, and fill our eyes with light.

SAMUEL LONGFELLOW

So you will go out with joy and be led out in peace.
The mountains and hills will burst into song before you,
and all the trees in the fields will clap their hands....
These things will be a reminder of the LORD's promise.

ISAIAH 55:12–13 NCV

A joyful heart is life itself, and rejoicing lengthens one's life.

ECCLESIASTICUS

But let all who take refuge in you rejoice; let them sing
joyful praises forever. Spread your protection over them,
that all who love your name may be filled with joy.

PSALM 5:11 NLT

Where others see but the dawn coming over the hill,
I see the soul of God shouting for joy.

WILLIAM BLAKE

He brought out his people with rejoicing,
his chosen ones with shouts of joy.

PSALM 105:43 NIV

*Those who run in the path of God's commands
have their hearts set free.*

Celebrate

Through all eternity to Thee a joyful song I'll raise;
for oh! eternity's too short to utter all Thy praise.

JOSEPH ADDISON

Rejoice! Celebrate all the good things that GOD, your God,
has given you and your family.

DEUTERONOMY 26:11 MSG

When I look at the galaxies on a clear night—when I look
at the incredible brilliance of creation, and think that this
is what God is like, then instead of feeling intimidated
and diminished by it, I am enlarged—
I rejoice that I am part of it.

MADELEINE L'ENGLE

Rejoice always, pray without ceasing, in everything give thanks;
for this is the will of God in Christ Jesus for you.

1 THESSALONIANS 5:16–18 NKJV

If we are cheerful and contented, all nature smiles...the flowers are
more fragrant, the birds sing more sweetly, and the sun,
moon, and stars all appear more beautiful,
and seem to rejoice with us.

ORISON SWETT MARDEN

*L*ive realistically. Give generously. Adapt willingly.
Trust fearlessly. Rejoice daily.

CHARLES SWINDOLL

Gratitude

It is right and good that we, for all things, at all times,
and in all places, give thanks and praise to You, O God.
We worship You, we confess to You, we praise You, we bless You,
we sing to You, and we give thanks to You: Maker, Nourisher,
Guardian, Healer, Lord, and Father of all.

LANCELOT ANDREWES

Enter his gates with thanksgiving;
go into his courts with praise.
Give thanks to him and praise his name.

PSALM 100:4 NLT

Happiness is a healthy mental attitude,
a grateful spirit, a clear heart full of love.

Gratitude. More aware of what you have than what you don't.
Recognizing the treasure in the simple—a child's hug, fertile soil,
a golden sunset. Relishing in the comfort of the common—
a warm bed, a hot meal, a clean shirt.

MAX LUCADO

Give thanks to the LORD and proclaim his greatness.
Let the whole world know what he has done.

1 CHRONICLES 16:8 NLT

I would maintain that thanks are the highest form of thought,
and that gratitude is happiness doubled by wonder.

G. K. CHESTERTON

Hidden Treasures

If we are children of God, we have a tremendous treasure
in nature and will realize that it is holy and sacred. We will see
God reaching out to us in every wind that blows,
every sunrise and sunset, every cloud in the sky,
every flower that blooms, and every leaf that fades.

OSWALD CHAMBERS

I'll lead you to buried treasures, secret caches of valuables—
Confirmations that it is, in fact, I, God...who calls you by your name.

ISAIAH 45:3 MSG

Jesus Christ opens wide the doors of the treasure house
of God's promises, and bids us go in and take with boldness
the riches that are ours.

CORRIE TEN BOOM

Blessed be the God and Father of our Lord Jesus Christ,
who has blessed us with every spiritual blessing
in the heavenly places in Christ.

EPHESIANS 1:3 NASB

God's gifts make us truly wealthy.
His loving supply never shall leave us wanting.

BECKY LAIRD

I rejoice in your word like one who discovers a great treasure.

PSALM 119:162 NLT

His Alluring Love

Late have I loved You,
O beauty so ancient and so new.
Late have I loved You!
You were within me while I
have gone outside to seek You.
Unlovely myself, I rushed towards
all those lovely things You had made.
And always You were with me.

AUGUSTINE

All the world is an utterance of the Almighty. Its countless beauties,
its exquisite adaptations, all speak to you of Him.

PHILLIPS BROOKS

May God give you eyes to see beauty
only the heart can understand.

Be still, and in the quiet moments, listen to the voice
of your heavenly Father. His words can renew your spirit...
no one knows you and your needs like He does.

JANET L. WEAVER SMITH

The joyful birds prolong the strain,
their song with every spring renewed;
the air we breathe, and falling rain,
each softly whispers: God is good.

JOHN HAMPDEN GURNEY

The LORD your God is with you.... He will take great delight in you,
he will quiet you with his love, he will rejoice over you with singing.

ZEPHANIAH 3:17 NIV

God Waits for Us

God is waiting for us to come to Him with our needs....
God's throne room is always open.

CHARLES STANLEY

The Lord is not slow in doing what he promised—the way some
people understand slowness. But God is being patient with you.

2 PETER 3:9 NCV

God waits to give to those who ask Him a wisdom that will
bind us to Himself, a wisdom that will find expression
in a spirit of faith and a life of faithfulness.

J. I. PACKER

God wants us to look to Jesus, the author and finisher of our faith.
He has already overcome similar trials and tribulations and will
give us the power to do the same. He waits only to be asked.

BILLY GRAHAM

Behold, this is our God; we have waited for him,
that he might save us. This is the LORD; we have waited for him;
let us be glad and rejoice in his salvation.

ISAIAH 25:9 ESV

God waits for us in the inner sanctuary of the soul.
He welcomes us there.

RICHARD J. FOSTER

Wonderful Love

Among our treasures are such wonderful things as the grace
of Christ, the love of Christ, the joy and peace of Christ.

L. B. COWMAN

Show the wonder of your great love.... Keep me as the apple
of your eye; hide me in the shadow of your wings.

PSALM 17:7–8 NIV

Every one of us as human beings is known and loved
by the Creator apart from every other human on earth.

JAMES DOBSON

The LORD is good to everyone;
he is merciful to all he has made.
LORD, everything you have made will praise you;
those who belong to you will bless you.
They will tell about the glory of your kingdom
and will speak about your power.
Then everyone will know the mighty things you do.

PSALM 145:9–12 NCV

The secret of the mystery is: God is always greater.
No matter how great we think Him to be,
His love is always greater.

BRENNAN MANNING

Give thanks to the LORD, for he is good!
His faithful love endures forever.

PSALM 136:1 NLT

Faithful Guide

So keep a firm grip on the faith.... It won't be long
before this generous God who has great plans for us in Christ—
eternal and glorious plans they are!—will have you put together
and on your feet for good. He gets the last word; yes, he does.

1 PETER 5:8–10 MSG

God, who has led you safely on so far, will lead you on to the end.
Be altogether at rest in the loving holy confidence which you ought
to have in His heavenly Providence.

FRANCIS DE SALES

The Lord leads with unfailing love and faithfulness
all who keep his covenant.

PSALM 25:10 NLT

God shall be my hope, my stay, my guide and lantern to my feet.

WILLIAM SHAKESPEARE

I am always with you; you hold me by my right hand. You guide me
with your counsel, and afterward you will take me into glory.

PSALM 73:23–24 NIV

*L*ive out your God-created identity. Live generously
and graciously toward others, the way God lives toward you.

MATTHEW 5:48 MSG

The Real Gift

This is the real gift: you have been given the breath of life,
designed with a unique, one-of-a-kind soul that exists forever....
Priceless in value, you are handcrafted by God,
who has a personal design and plan for each of us.

WENDY MOORE

Whether you turn to the right or to the left, your ears will hear a
voice behind you, saying, "This is the way; walk in it."

ISAIAH 30:21 NIV

Out of your relationship with God come life's greatest treasures—
fellowship, wisdom, peacefulness of soul, eternal hope, gladness of
heart, direction and meaning, and a glorious purpose in all you do.

ROY LESSIN

May he give you the desire of your heart
and make all your plans succeed.

PSALM 20:4 NIV

Allow your dreams a place in your prayers and plans. God-given
dreams can help you move into the future He is preparing for you.

What a joyful thought to realize you are a chosen vessel for God—
perfectly suited for His use.

JONI EARECKSON TADA

May God's love guide you through
the special plans He has for your life.

Ellie Claire™ Gift & Paper Corp.
Minneapolis, MN 55438
www.ellieclaire.com

This Is the Day...
Promise Journal
© 2010 by Ellie Claire™ Gift & Paper Corp.

ISBN 978-1-60936-010-8

Compiled by Jaymie Tomlinson
Cover and interior design by Lisa and Jeff Franke

Printed in China.